How Did Women and Children Live during the Civil War?

US History 5th Grade

Children's American History

Speedy Publishing LLC

40 E. Main St. #1156

Newark, DE 19711

www.speedypublishing.com

Copyright 2017

The American Civil War took place between the northern states and the southern states. The southern states did not like the idea of the North makings laws they did not like and instructing them as to what to do. Consequently, most of the southern states made a decision to split from the United States and formed the Confederacy. However, the North wanted to remain a united country; and then the war began. Including events leading up to the war, it lasted from 1860 to 1865.

American Civil War

During this war, the life of the soldier was difficult. In addition to facing the possibility of being killed during battle, their everyday lives were also full of hardship in dealing with boredom between battles, poor clothing, bad weather, and hunger.

The American Civil War affected the lives of everyone in the United States. While you may think of it as affected the soldiers at war, it also affected the lives of women and children.

Battle of Chickamauga

WHAT WAS LIFE LIKE DURING THE CIVIL WAR?

During the 1800s, life was difficult for almost everyone. While there were rich factory owners living in the North, and there were plantation owners in the South, the average farmer and their family had to work extremely hard to survive. Once the Civil War began, it became even more difficult to live for the average American. Most of the men had joined the army or had been drafted and the women had to take care of the household to support the family.

Women had to take care of the household as well as supplying the soldiers, providing their medical care, and they also worked as spies. Some even fought like the soldiers.

Children sometimes served as soldiers, and others witnessed the war's horror from afar. They had to become adults quickly, taking on new duties either at home or at the battleground.

LIFE AT HOME

Managing the Homestead – While the men were at war, the women had to manage their homes. This sometimes would include taking care of the businesses or farms that had been left behind by their husbands while they were at war.

RAISING MONEY

They also had to raise money to support the war. They would have raffles and fairs and the money would be used to pay for the war supplies.

TAKING ON MEN'S JOBS

Many of them had to take on jobs typically done by a man. They would work in government positions as well as in factories to fill positions that had been left behind by the men that were now at war. On a positive note, this changed the way that people perceived women's roles in society and helped progress the women's rights movement.

CARING FOR SOLDIERS AT CAMP

They also helped with caring for the soldiers as they camped and got ready for battle. They would sew their uniforms, provide them with blankets, mend their shoes, wash their clothes, and cook for them.

NURSES

Providing medical care for the wounded and sick soldiers became one of the most important roles they would play during this war. Many women would work as nurses. Dorothea Dix and Clara Barton organized the nursing and relief efforts. They assisted the doctors as needed, kept the soldiers' bandages clean, and fed the sick.

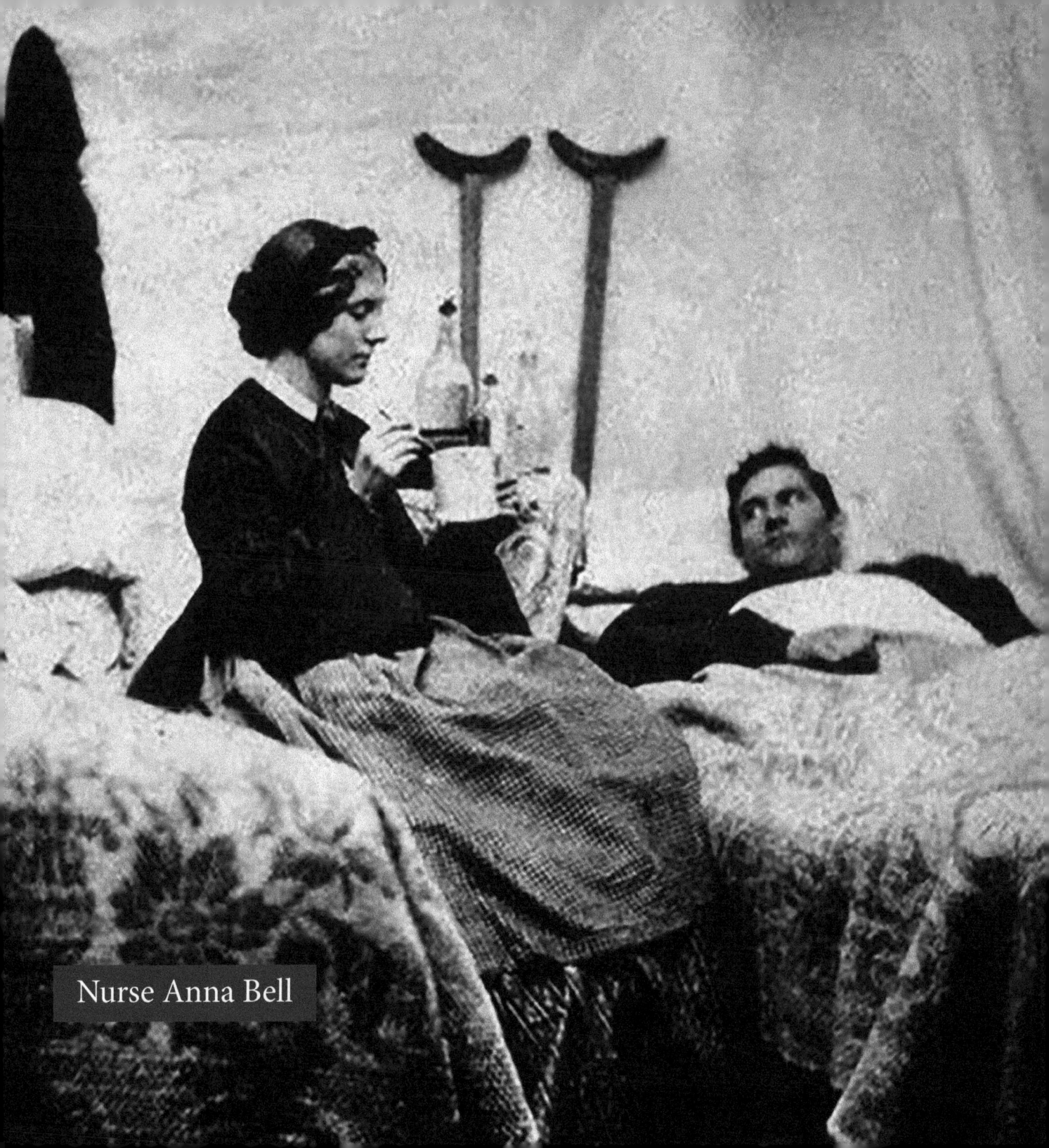

Nurse Anna Bell

Dorothea Dix

Dorothea Dix initially required the female nurses be older than 30. Louisa May Alcott, who authored Little Women, was a nurse for the Union.

The only woman that worked officially as a Union doctor was Mary Walker. At one time, she was captured by the South, but later was freed and went on to earn the Congressional Medal of Honor.

Mary Walker

SPIES

Women became some of the better spies for each side. Typically, they would be women that worked or lived on one side, and secretly supported the opposing side. This also included the slave women from the North that would support the South and then would provide information about the troop movements to the North. They would also include women in the North that supported the South and were then able to convince officers to provide them with vital information that would assist the South. They would even have spy rings they managed at home and would deliver information they received from the local spies.

WOMEN AS SOLDIERS

Even though they were not permitted to fight as soldiers, many managed to enter the army and fight the war. They would disguise themselves as a man. They wore bulky clothes and cut their hair. Soldiers would rarely change their clothes or bathe, and slept in their clothes so they were able to be undetected and would fight right alongside the men for a long time. If they were discovered, they would typically be sent home with no punishment. Over 400 women disguised as men were able to successfully fight in the war.

INFLUENTIAL WOMEN

Clara Barton

CLARA BARTON

She was a nurse during the Civil War and established the American Red Cross. She said that this war advanced women's rights by 50 years.

DOROTHEA DIX

She was the Union's Superintendent of Army Nurses. She became an activist for the mentally challenged.

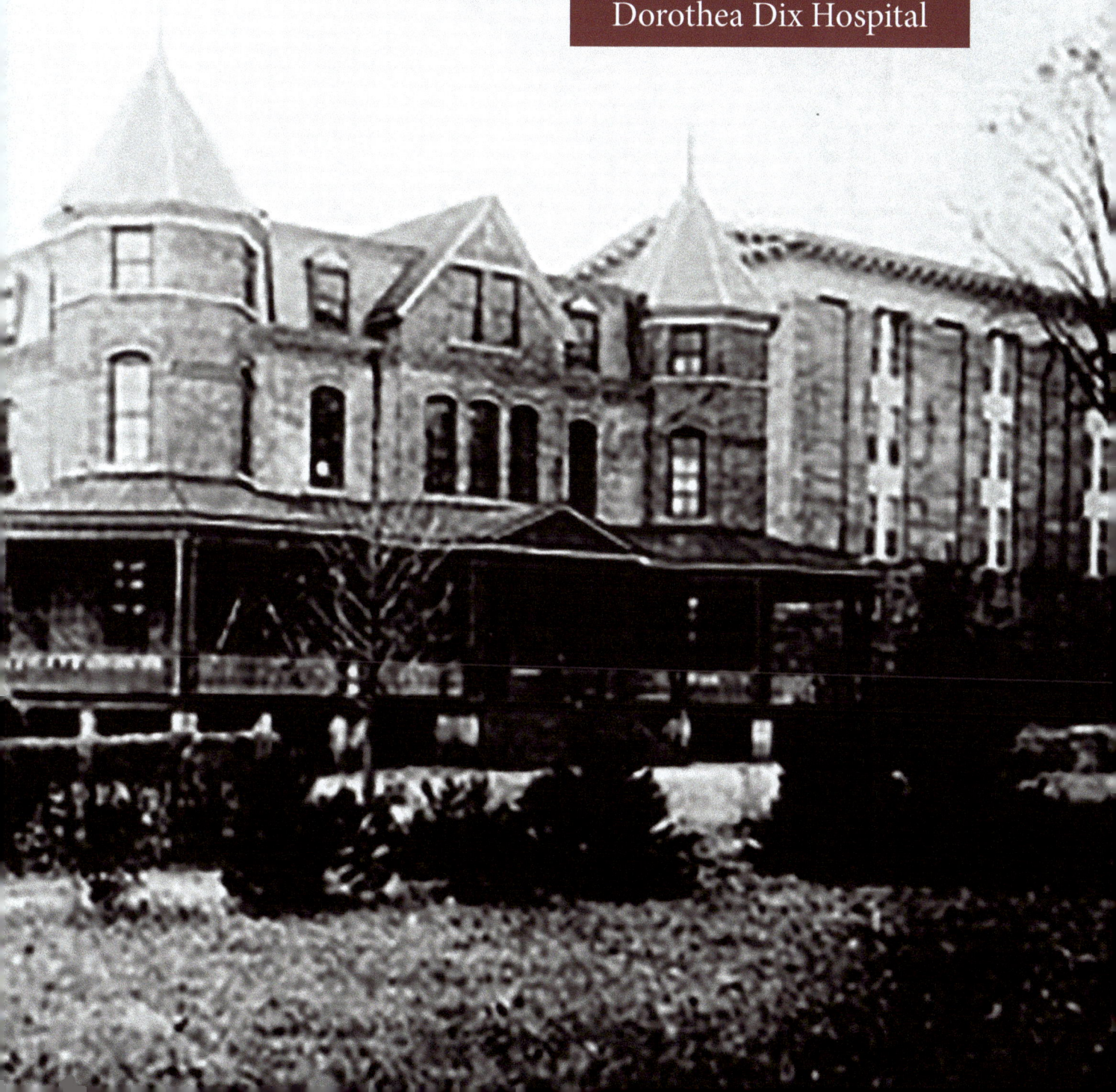

Dorothea Dix Hospital

Elizabeth Cady Stanton

ELIZABETH CADY STANTON

She fought to end slavery and fought for women's rights.

HARRIET BEECHER STOWE

She wrote Uncle Tom's Cabin exposing to the North exactly how harsh slavery was.

Henry Ward Beecher and Harriet Beecher Stowe

Harriet Tubman

HARRIET TUBMAN

She was a slave that escaped and worked with the Underground Railroad and went on to be a Union spy.

THE CHILDREN

The children attended school during the War, however, most of what they were taught was information instilling patriotisms either towards the Confederacy or the Union

USS Hunchback crewmen

BOYS IN THE ARMY

Even though soldiers in the war were supposed to be over 18, both sides desperately needed soldiers and decided to ignore the age issue. Consequently, more than a thousand boys fought this war that were between the ages of 13 and 17. Many of these young boys lost their lives or ended up wounded from battle.

They would sometimes place a note with 18 written on it in their shoes when they applied to be a soldier. This way they would not be lying when they said "I'm over 18".

The Civil War was often referred to as "The Boys' War" since many young boys became soldiers. It is estimated that up to 20% of the soldiers fighting this war were under 18.

DRUMMER BOYS AND MESSENGERS

The younger boys as soldiers typically ended up as messengers or drummers. Boys even at 10 years old are known to have served as drummers. Drummers provided communication on the battlefield. The different drum rolls would provide signals for different commands such as "attack" or "retreat". Other boys became messengers. Typically, they would be fast runners and would bravely run urgent messages from a commander to another commander.

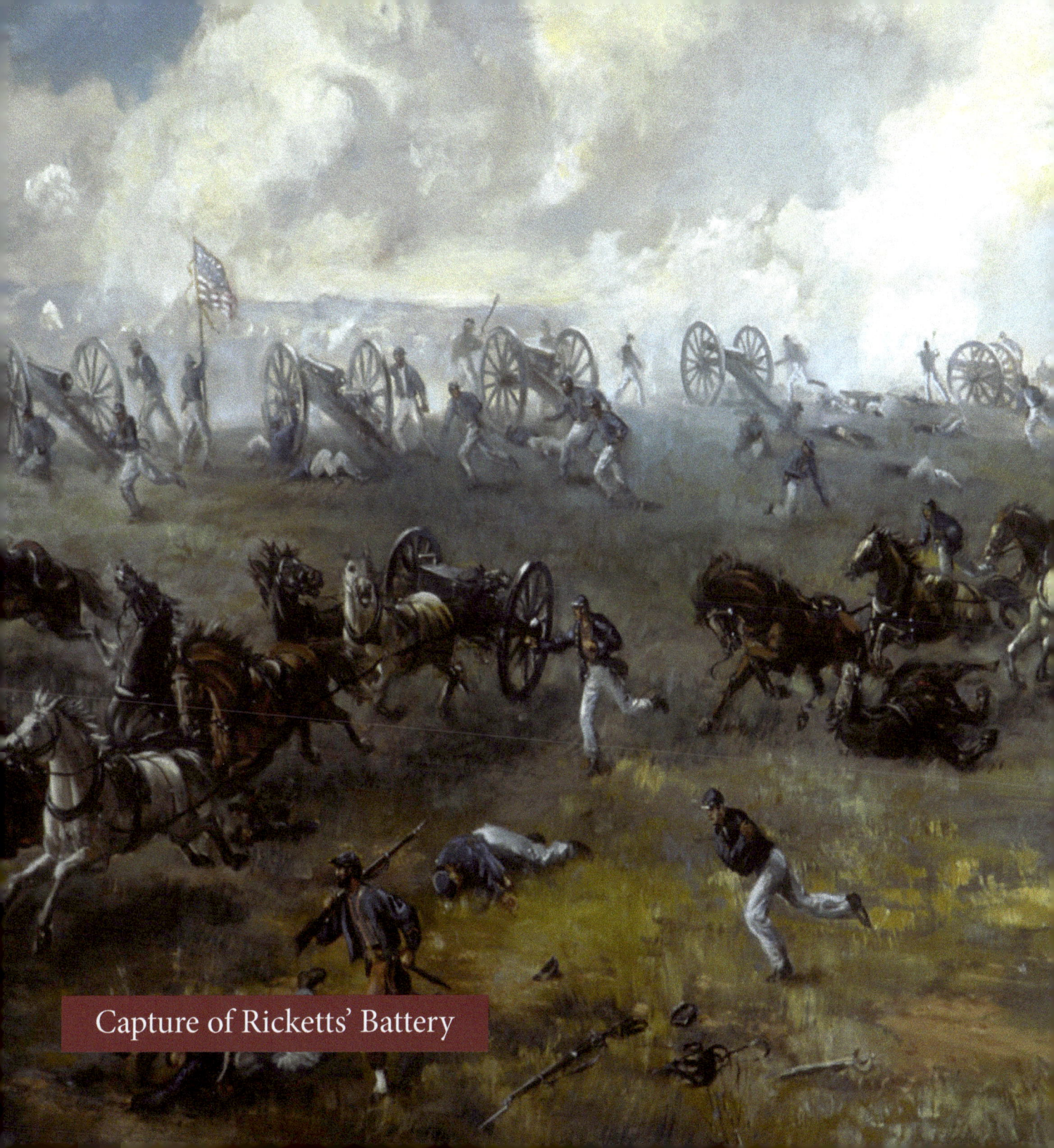

Capture of Ricketts' Battery

Johnny Clem

Johnny Clem was known to be the famous boy soldier of the Civil War. At the age of 9, he became the first boy to join the Union Army. He was then rejected due to his size and age. However, he refused to give up. He followed the 22nd Michigan regiment and they finally adopted him to be their drummer. When he was 13, he was finally able to join the Army. He then became famous for shooting a Confederate officer and proceeded to escape during the battle at Chickamauga, Georgia. His adventures during the war became legendary. After the war, he continued his work as a soldier and became Brigadier General. He became the last veteran of this war and retired in 1915 from the U.S. Armed Forces.

CHILDREN AT THE ARMY CAMPS

Many children worked in the camps, washing dishes, fixing meals, and setting up camp as they moved from place to place. They were not in as much danger as the soldiers, even though they were close to front lines.

Johnny Clem

Battle of Vicksburg

CHILDREN AT THE HOME

Life was not easy at home for the children either. Most of them had a relative off to war which might have been their father, brother, or their uncle. They often had to work extra and even had to take on adult jobs to help pay for household expenses. They also feared that their family may never return.

CHILDREN IN THE SOUTH

Living in the South created more fear since most of the fighting occurred there. If they lived near a battlefield, they could hear the gunshots and cannons going off throughout the night. They might also see the soldiers as they marched by going to battle or coming back from battle. They feared that enemy soldiers would destroy their homes or their crops.

Ruined buildings at Richmond

Battle of Chancellorsville

For additional information about life during the Civil War, research the internet, go to your local library, and ask questions of your teachers, family, and friends.

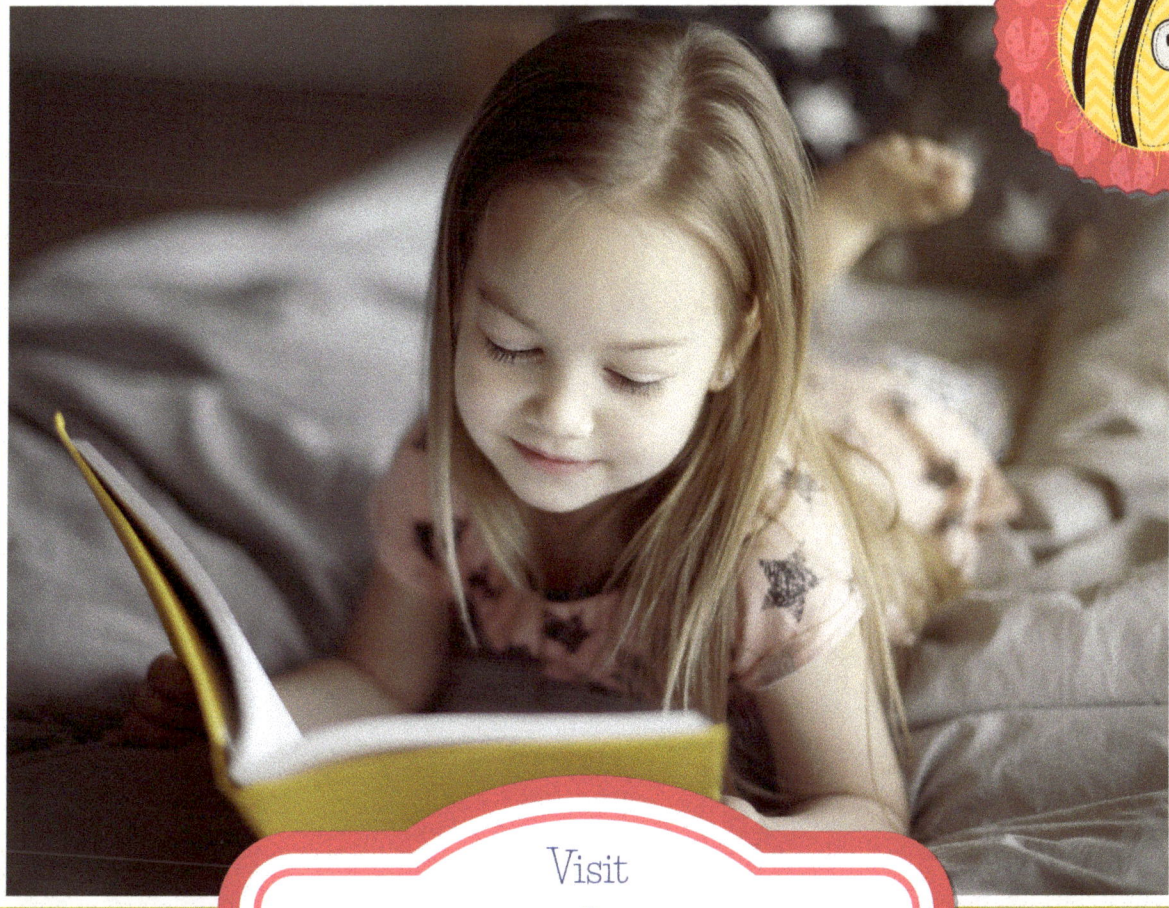

Visit

BABY PROFESSOR
EDUCATION KIDS

www.BabyProfessorBooks.com

to download Free Baby Professor eBooks
and view our catalog of new and exciting
Children's Books

Milton Keynes UK
Ingram Content Group UK Ltd.
UKHW051706030924
447642UK00002BA/74